Life Story of a
Ladybird

Charlotte Guillain

raintree
a Capstone company — publishers for children

Raintree is an imprint of Capstone Global Library Limited, a company incorporated in England and Wales having its registered office at 7 Pilgrim Street, London, EC4V 6LB – Registered company number: 6695582

www.raintreepublishers.co.uk
myorders@raintreepublishers.co.uk

Edited by Catherine Veitch and Gina Kammer
Designed by Richard Parker and Peggie Carley
Picture research by Mica Brancic
Production by Victoria Fitzgerald
Originated by Capstone Global Library Ltd
Printed and bound in China by Leo Paper Group

ISBN 978 1 406 28233 7 (hardback)
18 17 16 15 14
10 9 8 7 6 5 4 3 2 1

ISBN 978 1 406 28238 2 (paperback)
19 18 17 16 15
10 9 8 7 6 5 4 3 2 1

British Library Cataloguing in Publication Data
A full catalogue record for this book is available from the British Library.

Acknowledgements
We would like to thank the following for permission to reproduce photographs:

Ardea: Steve Hopkin, 20; FLPA: Gary K. Smith, 7, Matt Cole, 5, 21, Nigel Cattlin, 17, Phil McLean, 26; Nature Picture Library: Nature Production, 10; Photoshot: Jean-Claude Carton, 23; Science Source: E. R. Degginger, 16, Explorer, 25, Harry Rogers, 8, 28 (left), Mark Bowler, 18, Perennou Nuridsany, 9; Shutterstock: AlexussK (stone design element), cover and throughout, Christian Musat, 12, D. Kucharski and K. Kucharska, 11, 28 (right), Erik Mandre, 6, jannoon028 (grass border), throughout, ninii, cover, Pakhnyushcha, 19, Photo Fun, 13, Risto0, 27, Yellowj, 4, 29 (bottom), Yuliya Proskurina (green leaves border), cover and throughout; SuperStock: Biosphoto, 14, 15, 29 (top), 24, Juniors, 22

We would like to thank Michael Bright for his assistance in the preparation of this book.

Every effort has been made to contact copyright holders of material reproduced in this book. Any omissions will be rectified in subsequent printings if notice is given to the publisher.

Contents

Some words are shown in bold, **like this.** You can find out what they mean by looking in the glossary.

What is a ladybird?

A ladybird is a type of animal called an **insect**. Insects are animals with three pairs of legs and a body with three main parts. Many insects have wings.

Most ladybirds are less than a centimetre long. They usually have red or yellow covers over their wings with a spotted pattern.

A ladybird's life story

Like all animals, a ladybird goes through different stages as it grows into an adult. These stages make up an animal's life story.

adult ····>

young ····>

young

adult

Follow the life story of ladybirds and watch them change in unusual ways as they develop and grow.

It starts with an egg

A ladybird starts its life as an egg. The egg is tiny, smooth, and oval shaped. Some ladybird eggs are yellow.

A female ladybird lays her eggs under a leaf. The eggs are safe there from rain and from **predators** that might eat them.

The egg hatches

A ladybird **larva** hatches out of its egg after four to ten days.

Some ladybird larvae are grey and black with several body **segments**. Other ladybird larvae are brown or yellow.

A growing larva

A ladybird larva eats small insects, such as **aphids** or mites. It keeps eating and gets bigger and bigger.

A larva's skin splits four times as it grows bigger. Each time its skin splits, the larva crawls out with a new skin.

Changing into a pupa

After three to six weeks, the ladybird larva attaches itself to a leaf. Then it becomes a **pupa**.

A pupa stays still on the leaf for about two weeks. It is changing into an adult ladybird. This change of body shape is called **metamorphosis**.

Changing into an adult

When the pupa has changed into an adult ladybird, the skin splits open. An adult ladybird crawls out.

After a few hours, the ladybird's wing cases become a brighter colour and spots appear. The wing cases also become harder and dry out. Then the ladybird is ready to fly.

Like all insects, an adult ladybird has a pair of **antennae** on its head. The ladybird uses its antennae to smell, taste, and feel.

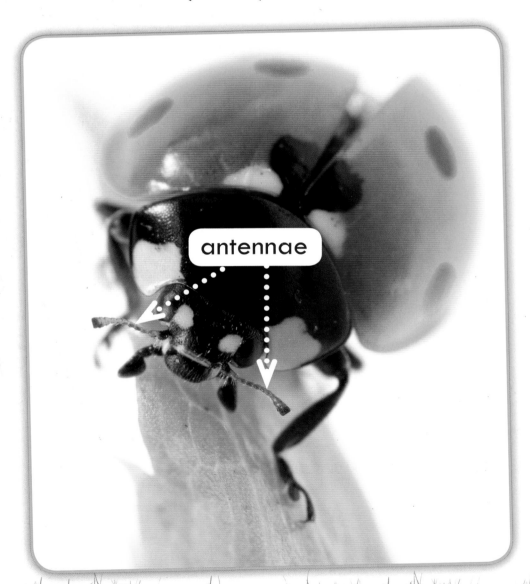

antennae

elytra

wings

The ladybird's wings are protected under spotted wing cases. These cases are called **elytra**.

A ladybird's bright colour is a warning to predators. The colour tells predators that it tastes nasty. A ladybird also makes a sticky substance when a predator attacks.

An adult ladybird mainly eats aphids. If
there aren't enough aphids, then the ladybird
might eat other ladybirds' larvae or eggs.

Mating

A ladybird looks for a mate so they can continue the life story. Together they can **reproduce** and create new ladybirds.

A male and female ladybird have to find
each other to mate. They release a special
smell when they are ready to find a mate.

After mating the female ladybird lays eggs on a plant leaf. She chooses a plant that is eaten by insects so that the larvae will have insects to eat when they hatch.

A female ladybird usually lays eggs in spring when plants are growing. After laying the eggs, it leaves.

A ladybird's life

Some ladybirds only live for a few months. Other ladybirds can live for about a year. Some ladybirds stay somewhere sheltered through the cold winter months.

Some animals and birds eat ladybirds.
When a ladybird dies, the ladybird life
story is continued by its young.

Ladybird life story diagram

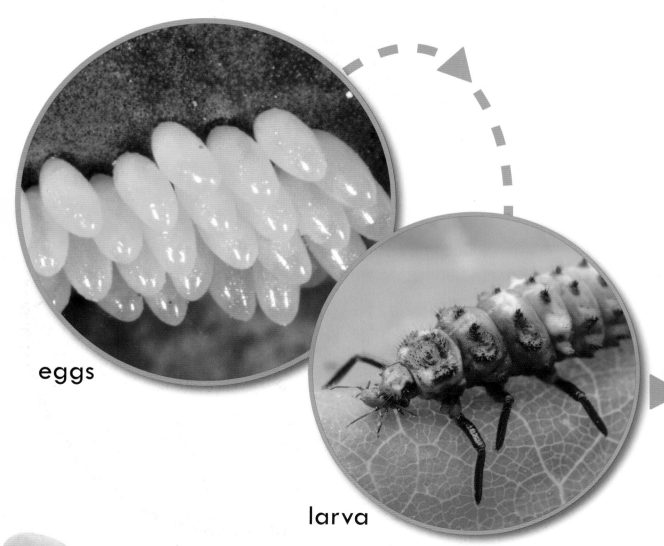

eggs

larva

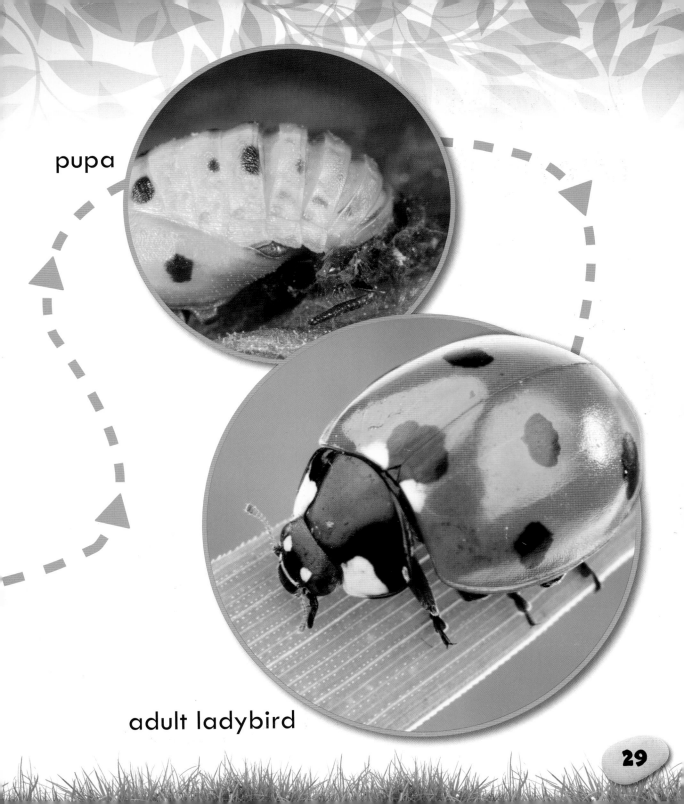

pupa

adult ladybird

29

Glossary

antennae long, thin feelers on an insect's head that it uses to feel and smell

aphid insect that sucks the juices of plants

elytra tough cases over a ladybird's delicate wings

insect type of animal with no backbone that has three main body parts and three pairs of legs

larva stage in an animal's life before it becomes an adult

metamorphosis stage where an animal changes body shape and appearance

predator animal that hunts and eats other animals

pupa the stage of an insect's life when it changes from a larva to an adult

reproduce to lay eggs or give birth to young

segment separate section

Find out more

Books

The Life Cycle of a Ladybird, Ruth Thomson
    (Hachette Children's Books, 2012)

Insects Sticker Book, Anthony Wootton
    (Usborne, 2010)

Websites

http://www.bbc.co.uk/nature/life/Coccinellidae
Visit the BBC Nature website to find out more about ladybirds and watch video clips.

http://www.arkive.org/seven-spot-ladybird/coccinella-septempunctata/image-A8736.html
The Arkive website has plenty of information and photos of the different stages of a ladybird's life.

Index